For anyone who struggles with a sense of belonging, of being seen and known, this is the devotional for you! The enemy wants to snuff out our God-given light, make us believe we are alone and unwanted, and then shackle us to his lies. Crystal Manget knows the enemy's tactics well as a lifelong warrior against the lie of shame. She vulnerably shares her story, with all its trials and suffering, and points her readers to God's pursuing and strengthening grace. Each daily devotional reminds the reader that God sees you, knows the truth of you, and loves you. Each daily devotional not only invites you into the truth of all that God is but gives you space to reflect, pray, and pause within the truth of Him. This beautifully tender book walks through the valley of life but is guided by the hope we have been given in Christ. As its title proclaims, God is a God of invitation. Come to His table and feast on the truth: You are a beloved, chosen, and altogether worthy child of God. Come to the table and exchange the ashes of shame for the beauty of His abundance. Come to the table and experience the freedom only found in Jesus Christ.

—Carol Belvin, Author of
Caught Up in Hope, *Caught Up in the Word*, and *You Are His*

Come to the Table is a beautifully written devotional that speaks directly to the soul of anyone held captive by the weight of shame. With biblical truth, grace, and courageous openness, Crystal draws us into a safe space in which to lay down the weight of our past and embrace our true identity in Christ. Her words are convicting yet comforting, and they offer a powerful reminder that we are never beyond the redemption of God, that He knows the depths of our hearts and loves us beyond what we could ever imagine. This devotional is for anyone longing to break free from the feelings of shame and journey toward the abundant life God has promised.

—Donna Bowles,
radio producer, KOOL 96.9 Birmingham

Come to the Table feels like a gentle, grace-filled conversation with a friend who's been through the fire and came out refined. Crystal shares herself and her experiences, not for sympathy but for transformation. She shares with honesty and deep compassion as she invites us to pull up a chair, clear the room of shame, and finally understand what God has been saying all along. You are seen, you are loved, and you belong at His table.

Her words feel like a warm cup of coffee with someone who gets it—someone who understands what it means to carry invisible wounds and still want to know Jesus more. Every page is an invitation to stop hiding behind past hurt and step fully into your God-given identity.

If you've ever felt overlooked, unworthy, or like you had to "fix yourself" before coming to Christ, this devotional will speak life into the places you've kept hidden. Crystal doesn't sugarcoat the journey but walks it with you, one truth-filled day at a time.

You will walk away from this thirty-day journey not just encouraged but changed.

—Christina Custodio,
author of *When God Changed His Mind*

30-Day Devotional

Come TO THE Table

A Shame-Free Invitation to Your Identity in Christ

You're Invited...
to see yourself as God does — Chosen — Loved

Crystal

30-Day Devotional

Come TO THE Table

A Shame-Free Invitation to Your Identity in Christ

CRYSTAL MANGET

Foreword by Athena Dean Holtz

© 2025 by Crystal Manget. All rights reserved.

Published by Redemption Press, 70 S. Val Vista Drive, Suite A3-422, Gilbert, AZ 85296, (360) 226-3488.

Redemption Press is honored to present this title in partnership with the author. The views expressed or implied in this work are those of the author. Redemption Press provides our imprint seal representing design excellence, creative content, and high-quality production.

Noncommercial interests may reproduce portions of this book without the express written permission of the author, provided the text does not exceed five hundred words. When reproducing text from this book, include the following credit line: "*Come to the Table* by Crystal Manget. Used by permission."

Commercial interests: No part of this publication may be reproduced in any form, stored in a retrieval system, or transmitted in any form by any means—electronic, photocopy, recording, or otherwise—without prior written permission of the publisher/author, except as provided by United States of America copyright law.

Unless otherwise indicated, all Scripture quotations are from The ESV® Bible (The Holy Bible, English Standard Version®), © 2001 by Crossway, a publishing ministry of Good News Publishers. Used by permission. All rights reserved.

Scripture quotations marked (KJV) are from the King James Version, public domain.

Scripture quotations marked (MSG) are taken from *The Message*, copyright © 1993, 2002, 2018 by Eugene H. Peterson. Used by permission of NavPress. All rights reserved. Represented by Tyndale House Publishers.

Scripture quotations marked (NIV) are taken from the Holy Bible, New International Version®, NIV®. Copyright © 1973, 1978, 1984, 2011 by Biblica, Inc.™ Used by permission of Zondervan. All rights reserved worldwide. www.zondervan.com. The "NIV" and "New International Version" are trademarks registered in the United States Patent and Trademark Office by Biblica, Inc.™

Scripture quotations marked (NLT) are taken from the *Holy Bible*, New Living Translation, copyright © 1996, 2004, 2015 by Tyndale House Foundation. Used by permission of Tyndale House Publishers, Carol Stream, Illinois 60188. All rights reserved.

ISBN 13: 978-1-64645-936-0 (paperback)

Library of Congress Catalog Card Number: 2025907218

*This devotional is dedicated
to all who feel worthless, devalued,
and possess a sense of hopelessness.*

*I see you because
I have been you.
There is hope.*

I define shame as the intensely painful feeling or experience of believing that we are flawed and therefore unworthy of love and belonging—something we've experienced, done, or failed to do makes us unworthy of connection.

—Brené Brown

Contents

- vii | Foreword
- ix | Acknowledgments
- 1 | Introduction
- 8 | Day 1: A New Creation
- 12 | Day 2: Accepted
- 16 | Day 3: Enough
- 20 | Day 4: Heard
- 23 | Day 5: Chosen
- 28 | Day 6: Masterpiece
- 32 | Day 7: Qualified
- 36 | Day 8: Forgiven
- 40 | Day 9: Loved
- 44 | Day 10: Known
- 48 | Day 11: Secure
- 52 | Day 12: Redeemed
- 56 | Day 13: Coheir of God
- 60 | Day 14: Never Alone

- 64 | Day 15: Treasured
- 68 | Day 16: Adopted
- 72 | Day 17: Equipped
- 76 | Day 18: Made Whole
- 80 | Day 19: Strong
- 84 | Day 20: Holy
- 88 | Day 21: Citizen of Heaven
- 92 | Day 22: Cared For
- 96 | Day 23: Reconciled
- 100 | Day 24: Valuable
- 104 | Day 25: More Than Conquerors
- 108 | Day 26: Child of God
- 112 | Day 27: Ambassador
- 116 | Day 28: Gifted
- 120 | Day 29: Free
- 124 | Day 30: Victorious
- 128 | Conclusion: Reframe Your Shame
- 132 | Questions for Digging Deeper
- 139 | Endnotes

Foreword

Shame is a quiet force—persistent, heavy, and too often undetected. It creeps into our hearts, whispers doubt into our minds, and distorts the truth of who we are. It convinces us that we are irreparably broken, unworthy of love, and disconnected from God. Yet, in His unwavering grace, God calls each of us into the light, where shame's lies are replaced with His truths.

Come to the Table: A Shame-Free Invitation to Your Identity in Christ is a deeply moving and hope-filled guide to that very transformation. Through the pages of this devotional, you'll join the author on her courageous and honest journey from a shame-based identity to one rooted in God's unshakable love. Her story is one of redemption and renewal, a testament to God's power to take our wounds and transform them into reflections of His grace.

With compassion and vulnerability, the author invites us to her table—a table piled high with the clutter of past wounds, self-doubt, and distorted perceptions. But as she helps us clear away the lies and burdens of shame, we begin to see what lies beneath—a beautiful, open space where we can meet Christ, fully seen and deeply loved.

This devotional isn't just a testimony; it's a guide to stepping into your God-given identity. Through carefully chosen Scripture, meaningful prayers, and personal reflection, the author equips you with tools to uncover the truth about who you are in Christ. Each passage points you to the cross, where shame was defeated once and for all. By walking alongside, you'll discover ways to release the burden of shame and experience the extraordinary freedom and purpose that come with living as the person God created you to be.

This book reminds us that in Christ, we are never too far gone, never too bruised, and never too broken to be made whole. With every devotional, you are encouraged to see yourself through God's eyes—pure, cherished, and wonderfully made. Truth replaces lies, self-compassion replaces harsh judgment, and joy fills the space once held by shame.

I encourage you to take these thirty days as a gift. Allow yourself to be vulnerable, to dig deep, and to trust God to heal even the places you've kept hidden. Lean into the author's reflections, and more importantly, lean into the truth of Scripture that she so beautifully weaves throughout her words.

Clear away the clutter, beloved. Christ is at the table, calling you to sit, to rest, and to know Him fully. Through this book, may you grasp the depth of His love and rediscover the remarkable identity He has given you, free from shame, rooted in grace, and radiant with purpose.

Come to the table and take your place as His beloved. You belong here.

—Athena Dean Holtz,
publisher, author, spiritual abuse survivor

Acknowledgments

This book would not be possible without the support of my husband, Jeff, the encouragement of my Monday night ladies and my friends Alison and Carol, and my personal cheerleader and daughter, Victoria.

A special thank you goes to my editors and project manager with Redemption Press.

Above all, I must express my gratitude to God, who gave me the idea for the book and the words written. He walked beside me through the most difficult chapters of my life so my story could speak His name and point others to Him.

Introduction

Picture this: a *large* banquet table set with beautiful china and a detailed ornate tablecloth. Seated at one end is Christ, and at the opposite end, you. Stretched out in between is a landscape of large platters, small bowls, and dishes of every size. But the beauty of the tablecloth underneath gets lost under all the clutter.

Now imagine picking up one of those many dishes and seeing a beautifully embroidered, God-given name. But just as quickly as you pick up that dish, you set it back down, as the dish is weighed down by shame. Even though your heart might long to be near to Jesus, the shame you carry creates an uncomfortable distance.

So how do you change your seat at the table? How do you fully embrace who you are in Christ? You must unpack the shame you carry and trade it for the freedom of your identity in Him.

For many, this begins with the hurt of our past, as our identity is normally tangled up in our day-to-day living: mother/father, daughter/son, wife/husband, job title, and other labels. However, who we are in our core often depends on how we were raised. Healthy self-esteem comes from a healthy upbringing. But an unhealthy upbringing can destroy self-esteem, often creating an identity rooted in shame. This is in every way my story.

From the outside looking in, my upbringing presented a picturesque happy family who came to church every time the doors were open. But behind closed doors, verbal abuse and shame ruled. I was the younger of two children and my older brother was the "chosen child," the standard to which I had to always measure up.

Sadly, I would never measure up. Self-doubt found a home in my mother's constant criticism. Phrases like "You are so stupid" plagued my childhood and created a negative soundtrack that would eventually lead me to attempt suicide. Shame convinced me that I was unworthy of life and love, but by His grace, God brought me healing and the ability to see others who were suffering the effects of shame.

A shame-based identity often leaves one feeling worthless, inferior, and disconnected. It can also make it difficult to trust others and move forward in life, which is the perfect place for isolation to take root. When we keep our lives bottled up, shame thrives. But by allowing godly women and men into our lives and sharing our stories, even those we hide out of fear, then we slowly release the effects shame has had on us.

When I accepted Christ as my Savior, I was taught that a change would be immediate and visible. While I understood there was a change inside, something kept me rooted in the past. The shame I carried prevented me from showing others the change I felt. At the time, my church was more concerned with teaching about our sin than who we are in Christ.

But then a shift happened. I began attending a new church. They started a series centered on our relationship with Christ and, therefore, the identity we have in Him. I have been able to cling to a few names that come with that identity, which resonated and removed the effects of my shame-based identity. Each time I understood a new name, I felt a burden lift.

This devotional is written with the vulnerability of my own story entwined with the truth of who we are in Christ. Hopefully it will confirm that you are not who others say you are (or who your negative tape says you are) but who God says you are. El Roi, the God who sees, sees us as we are: purified with the blood of Christ, holy, and pure. We were made new the day we accepted Christ as our Savior. So, let's change *our* heart's vision to *His* heart's vision together.

Hebrews 12:2 (KJV) says, "Looking unto Jesus the author and finisher of our faith; who for the joy that was set before him endured the cross, despising the shame, and is set down at the right hand of the throne of God."

PRAYER

If we ever doubt who we are in Jesus, we need only look at the words He prayed over us with His crucifixion looming. Even then, we were on His mind. Even then, He took His disciples before God's throne. Even then, He asked His loving Father to protect *us*, sanctify *us*, and let *us* feel the joy of who we are because we *belong* to Him.

Christ's prayer covers us in a love that is beyond anything this life could provide. It is love that offers hope. And it is in that hope, we begin.

Father, the hour has come; glorify your Son that the Son may glorify you, since you have given him authority over all flesh, to give eternal life to all whom you have given him. And this is eternal life, that they know you, the only true God, and Jesus Christ whom you have sent....

I am praying for them. I am not praying for the world but for those whom you have given me, for they are yours.... But now I am coming to you, and these things I speak in the world, that they may have my joy fulfilled in themselves.... I do not ask that you take them out of the world, but that you keep them from the evil one. Sanctify them in the truth; your word is truth....

I do not ask for these only, but also for those who will believe in me through their word, that they may all be one, just as you, Father, are in me, and I in you, that they also may be in us, so that the world may believe that you have sent me.... Father, I desire that they also, whom you have given me, may be with me where I am, to see my glory that you have given me because you loved me before the foundation of the world.

(John 17:1–3, 9, 13, 15, 17, 21, 24 ESV)

SELAH: AN INVITATION TO PAUSE

At the end of each devotion, you will have an opportunity to take a Selah moment before diving into the next day. Its meaning holds special weight as *Selah* is a Hebrew word inviting us to pause, underline, contemplate, transition, and/or listen. Also used as a musical notation to lift a collective voice of praise, this word and the practice it provides helps us keenly on the journey to dismantling shame. I recommend that after you read through the book, you go back and read the devotions again—this time journaling more deeply using the prompts in the conclusion. I pray each Selah moment provides an opportunity for you to pause and fully embrace each characteristic of your identity in Christ.

DAY 1
A New Creation

Therefore, if anyone is in Christ, he is a new creation. The old has passed away; behold, the new has come.
2 Corinthians 5:17

"You could be so pretty…" My mother's disdainful words still echo across my teenage years, a time when I often felt devalued and unloved. Even though I became a Christian at the age of eleven, I did not fully understand what a relationship with Christ looked like. And it was hard to see myself as a new creation, especially when I was plagued by shame at home.

When I entered college, shame made it easier to give myself away to the first guy who noticed me. I thought by giving in to a moment of passion, I would feel valued and loved. But shame filled me instead. And each time I tried to walk closely with God and make better choices, shame told me there was no use trying to change, and I believed God couldn't love me because of the things I had done.

Even as I was studying my identity in Christ, I discovered I was still holding on to shame—shame about my appearance, intelligence, and choices I had made. But then I began to see that *in* Christ, there is no place for shame, and I slowly started sharing my shame-filled story, revealing things I had long kept hidden from others. By being vulnerable in sharing my story, I was able to start overcoming shame's grip on me. Vulnerability allowed others to find themselves in *my* story. The lasting effects that shame had on me have written a powerful story that only God could pen.

Even the phrase "the old has passed away" directs us to who we were before we accepted Christ. Everything we *were*, including our shame, died the minute we believed that Jesus died for our sins. Shame wants us to believe that there is something inside us that could not die on that cross. And for some of us, that lie is all-consuming. We hold on to it until our self-worth starts to crumble, and then we believe there is no way God could love us.

But if we believe Christ died on the cross for our sins, then the old way of thinking about life changes. We can enter into a new way of thinking by believing in the sufficiency of His work on the cross. Yes, it is that simple. We've been made new, no longer bound by the old. Those binds that fill us with shame were cut the moment Jesus uttered the words "It is finished."

AN INVITATION TO REFLECT

- ❖ What does the name "New Creation" mean to you right now?
- ❖ How is shame keeping you from embracing who you are as a new creation in Christ?
- ❖ How can accepting the name "New Creation" reframe your relationship with Jesus?

AN INVITATION TO PRAY

Abba Father, to be made new is difficult for me to grasp as I still see myself through the cracked lens of shame. Redirect my thoughts so they reflect my new identity in You. Show me how

You created me to be something more than my shame can see. Remove any stumbling blocks and give me the courage to embrace that You covered my shame on the cross once and for all. Amen.

AN INVITATION TO PAUSE

How does understanding this characteristic of your identity in Christ change your place setting at the table?

My Notes

DAY 2

Accepted

*Accept one another, then, just as Christ accepted you,
in order to bring praise to God.*
Romans 15:7 (NIV)

Shame had me constantly looking outside of my peers and my family for affirmation, but I found out quickly that being surrounded does not always make you feel accepted. I felt the sting of rejection many times, but in my family, I also felt it in subtle ways. It ran so deeply that even my mother's calling my brother "son" pained me. To me it felt as if she was calling him "sun." Her world revolved around him, and I would always be in his shadow.

When he died, she was asked a few years later to share her testimony. She gave me the video tape of the church service for me to watch afterward as I was not invited to hear it live. In her speech, she shared her life story, and as per usual, it was mostly about him. Had you not known she had two children, you would have assumed my brother was an only child. Once again, I came away rejected and devalued, which led me to seek acceptance outside my world.

Scripture tells us about God and His love for us, but acceptance often feels a bit harder to embrace. And yet, because God loves us, we are accepted into His presence through Christ. This means we have a place; we belong to that place by design.

People are broken, selfish, and often inconsiderate of one another's feelings, but God is not. He knows what it is to be rejected by people who are broken, who inflict hurt because they are hurt, and who only want what is best for themselves. And yet, God wants what is best for us, giving us each a place in this world and, more importantly, a place with Him.

AN INVITATION TO REFLECT

- ❖ What does the name "Accepted" mean to you right now?
- ❖ How is shame keeping you from embracing the freedom of being accepted by God?
- ❖ How can living fully within His acceptance reframe your relationship with Jesus and with others?

AN INVITATION TO PRAY

Abba Father, what an amazing truth that You loved me and accepted me before even I came to be. I am humbled at that very thought. My heart sings Your praises, for You alone are worthy. Thank You for all the ways the Scriptures affirm how much You love me. Amen.

AN INVITATION TO PAUSE

How does understanding this characteristic of your identity in Christ change your place setting at the table?

My Notes

DAY 3

Enough

Each time he said, "My grace is all you need.
My power works best in weakness."
2 Corinthians 12:9 (NLT)

How can I ever measure up to the standards my brother established as the perfect child? How can I be enough for anyone, let alone God? Driven by my fear of the standards established by my older brother, these thoughts took root and began a lifelong battle with perfectionism. Seeking the approval of my mother and using my brother as my measuring tool, I could only see my shortcomings due to comparison, a tool that can often keep a person stuck in a negatively focused state.

When we have been raised in an environment that was ubercritical, then perfectionism can take root. Perfection is unobtainable, and no matter how hard you strive, failure will happen at some point. Because I was made to feel that others were better than me, their opinion mattered more than mine, and they could see things I could not, I found myself believing I was also a failure. Alone in a world of comparison, I could not understand being enough for God.

The actual definition of enough is "as much or as many as required." Combine that with the feeling of being alone, and shame is left to rule and prevent us from seeing ourselves as God does. We need the spiritual strength that Christ provides and His eyes to see us as we are *in* Him. *Alone* only feeds the negative tape playing in our minds, the one that says we are never enough.

Building our identities on who Scripture says we are in Christ is like building a house. A house built on shame is a shaky dark shack that cannot withstand the storms of life. A house filled with shame can only focus on failures and is, therefore, unable to be enough for anyone, especially God. A house built on a firm foundation of Scripture is a house that can not only withstand those storms but one that can be a beacon for others. By studying the identity we have in Christ, we will be able to change the shame-filled house to one that is filled with God's light because we are enough.

AN INVITATION TO REFLECT

- ❖ What does the name "Enough" mean to you right now?
- ❖ How is shame keeping you from being enough in Christ?
- ❖ How do you think the name "Enough" can reframe who you think you are in Christ?

AN INVITATION TO PRAY

Abba Father, am I really enough for You? I need You to show me *how*. Insecurities plague me and I fail to see how I can be adequate. Shift my focus to how You see me, insecurities and all. Lord, change the words I carry that have made me want to be *perfect* to *enough*. Fill me with Your light—the one that says I am loved, valued, and worthy. Amen.

AN INVITATION TO PAUSE

How does understanding this characteristic of your identity in Christ change your place setting at the table?

My Notes

DAY 4

Heard

*I love the LORD, because he has heard my voice
and my pleas for mercy. Because he inclined his ear to me.*
Psalm 116:1–2

As a child, I longed to be deeply connected with others. I thought the only way to do that was through conversation. However, instead of being heard, I received statements like "Children should be seen and not heard" or "Where's the off button?" These responses made me feel like I was unimportant. From a childhood filled with negative comments about talking too much, it is refreshing and encouraging to know God not only wants to hear from me, but He actually bends down to hear me.

Once I understood that God wouldn't tell me to shut up constantly as others did, I could embrace His call to be still. And as I did so, I could hear Him asking me to seek Him with all my heart. I could hear Him asking me to unburden myself. As a result, He lifted my shame and opened His arms to welcome me into freedom.

For someone who was made to feel smaller by adults not wanting to engage in a deeper relationship with authentic conversation, that freedom was crucial in seeing myself as God sees me. It established that God wants a deeper connection with me through studying His Word, being still, and spending time in prayer.

When we seek Him, we get to hear His voice. When we pray, He hears our voice. And when we enter daily into relationship with Him, He is able to release the shame we feel and trade it for a new identity rooted deeply in His love.

AN INVITATION TO REFLECT

- ❖ What does knowing you are heard mean to you right now?
- ❖ How is shame keeping you silenced and from being heard by God?
- ❖ How do you think embracing the name "Heard" can reframe who you think you are in Christ?

AN INVITATION TO PRAY

Abba Father, I sit before You with an open heart and mind, desiring to seek You above all others. Being heard by You is like a warm blanket wrapping around my shame-filled heart. I ask You to take that shame I have been made to feel and replace it with the knowledge that You hear the cry of my heart. Lord, I long to be deeply connected with You. Bless me with a connection that cannot be interrupted. I pray this in Your holy name. Amen.

AN INVITATION TO PAUSE

How does understanding this characteristic of your identity in Christ change your place setting at the table?

My Notes

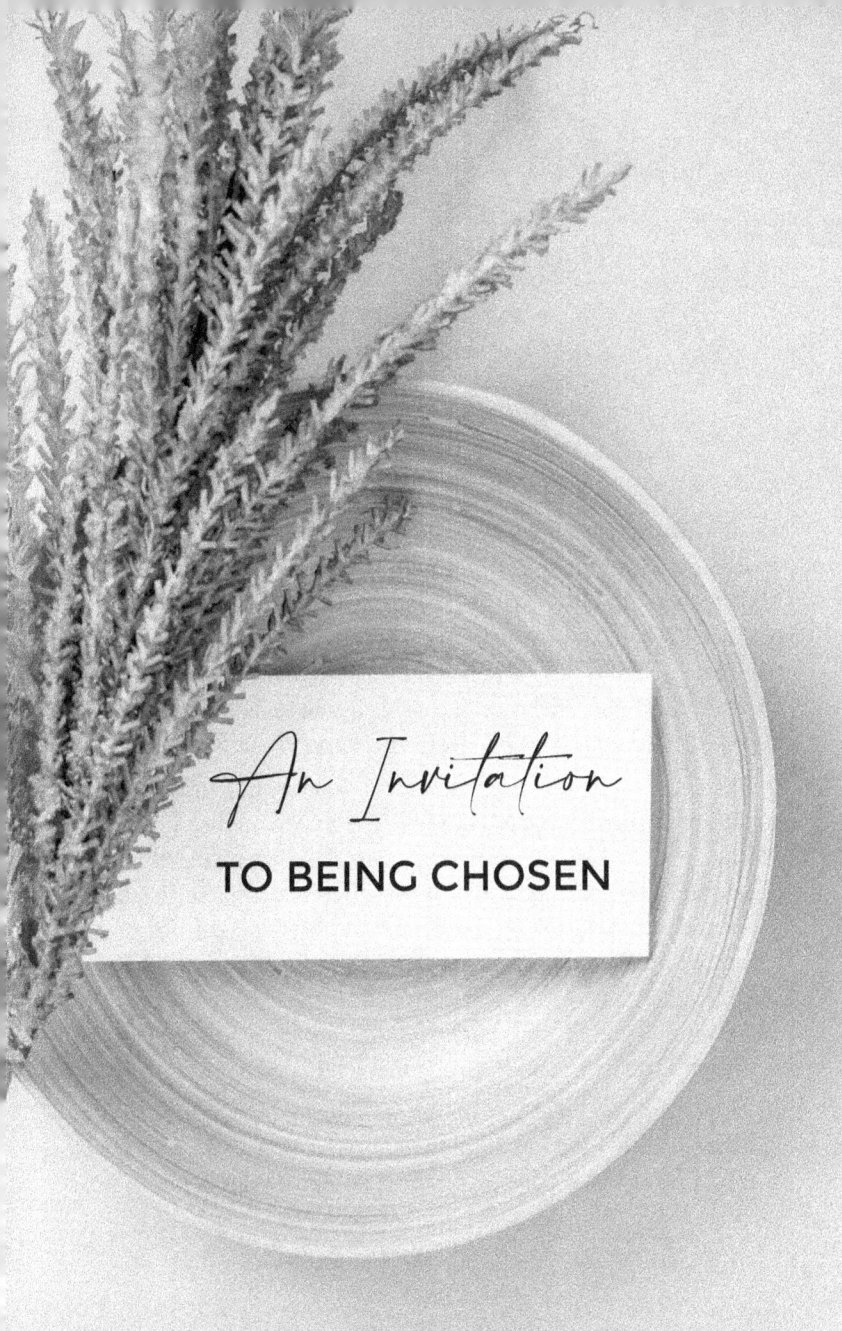

DAY 5

Chosen

> *"You did not choose me, but I chose you
> and appointed you that you should go and bear fruit
> and that your fruit should abide,
> so that whatever you ask the Father in my name,
> he may give it to you."*
> John 15:16

Having not experienced the grace of growing up feeling chosen made accepting I was chosen by God all the more difficult. My brother was the one everyone wanted around. My mother preferred his company. Teachers preferred him and would often tell me I needed to be more like him. No matter how desperately I wanted to be chosen by my mother or showered with the same approval she readily gave my brother, it never seemed to happen.

But it also meant that in Christ, I found one characteristic I could understand—being chosen by someone who loved me. Finally, I could experience what it was like. Just saying the word some days allowed me to feel God's presence. Shame hated this name and kept whispering the lies I had experienced from others: "Your brother is the chosen one; you will never be." When I bought into the lie, I kept myself away from others. Self-preservation said it was easier to not experience the pain of rejection. That fear remains strong in my life.

Over the years, the fear of rejection helped me engage in false narratives. I felt I did not have friends, so I often I rejected friends before they could reject me. It was a practice I developed out of harsh words from my mother about friends in my childhood. Looking back, I saw that I had already started isolating myself in grade school.

When we feel unsafe, we look for ways to feel safe. For me, it was to become somewhat invisible, and in time, I became a master at it. But being chosen by God fights against that need. The truth is He calls out to us, "Come to me." And we can trust He will embrace us with a sense of comfort and security no matter how others might treat us.

AN INVITATION TO REFLECT

- ❖ What does the name "Chosen" mean to you right now?
- ❖ How is shame keeping you from embracing the love being chosen offers?
- ❖ How can embracing the name "Chosen" reframe your shame identity?

AN INVITATION TO PRAY

Abba Father, You chose me before I could understand what it meant to be chosen. You chose me and, in doing so, made me feel loved and secure. Help me remember Your choice when my insecurity flares. May I remember to be thankful for all the ways You've chosen me. Amen.

AN INVITATION TO PAUSE

How does understanding this characteristic of your identity in Christ change your place setting at the table?

My Notes

DAY 6

Masterpiece

> *We are God's masterpiece.*
> *He has created us anew in Christ Jesus,*
> *so we can do the good things he planned for us long ago.*
> Ephesians 2:10 NLT

When we consider some of the greatest human-made masterpieces, the artistry in this God-given name is unmistakable. Having been to Paris and seen sculptures by Michaelangelo, I know each chisel placement results in a beautiful outcome. The same goes for *Mona Lisa* and *The Last Supper*. Each brush stroke of the artist comes together to create a painted masterpiece. But none of these works compare to us, God's masterpieces. Think about that for a second. The way each vein runs through the body, carrying blood and oxygen to various places it's needed is a beautiful design. Each part of the body comes together to form a one-of-a-kind masterpiece.

Consider our fingerprints as well. No two are alike. The same holds true for each one of us. God knits our pieces together to create something for which there is no mold. Shame tells us we are misfits, not belonging anywhere, but God says we are *His* masterpieces. What beauty there is in being called a masterpiece, especially for those of us who struggle to believe we are beautiful.

Not only are we masterpieces, but we also serve a purpose He created just for us. Shame can try to tell us that we are worthless and we don't belong, but this identity says otherwise.

Being God's masterpiece offers us a value that can only come from the Creator. As a creator, He took the time to plan who we would be before we were. He planned every part of us. He even knew we would need reassurance in the names He gives us.

AN INVITATION TO REFLECT

- ❖ What does the name "Masterpiece" mean to you right now?
- ❖ How is shame keeping you from embracing the beauty of being a masterpiece?
- ❖ How can being called a "masterpiece" reframe your shame identity?

AN INVITATION TO PRAY

Abba Father, I see the beauty of Your handiwork and I know that You created some amazing things on this earth. The fact that You consider me a masterpiece humbles me. Help me see myself as Your unique masterpiece. Thank You for seeing me not as I see myself but as something beautiful. Amen.

AN INVITATION TO PAUSE

How does understanding this characteristic of your identity in Christ change your place setting at the table?

My Notes

DAY 7

Qualified

Giving thanks to the Father, who has qualified you to share in the inheritance of the saints in light.
Colossians 1:12

What makes a person qualified? And for what are they qualified? When interviewing for a position in a company, the interviewer will often ask questions relating to the qualifications of the interviewee. The right questions extract answers that determine the best candidate for the job.

So how can we see that we are qualified in Christ? By asking the right questions, we can better explore this idea of being qualified and identify where shame extracts the wrong assumptions. *Are you in Christ?* This simple question speaks to the height of your faith. *Do you believe in Christ? Understand who He is? Know that He died for our sins? Rose from the grave?* All of these questions should have the same answer: yes.

When we become Christ followers, that qualifies us to be a part of God's family. Not just a part, but as we will see in the coming days, total coheirs with Christ and fully beloved children of God. This act of faith opens all God-breathed identities to each of us. Faith, not works, qualifies us as saints. Faith qualifies us to call God "Abba Father." Faith is the answer to any question or false statement that shame brings to the table.

Shame develops a personality when we take hurtful statements from others to heart. Those statements distort the truth about who we are. Shame continues to tell us those false statements each time we try to change our mindset. For me, shame whispers several lies that feed doubt. When doubt kicks in, then I shut down. When I shut down, then I spiral into a negative-obsessed thought process. I've learned to call it a *why wheel*. It is like a hamster wheel that goes nowhere fast. In the end, I am exhausted and depressed, full of self-doubt and self-loathing. When faith kicks in, I am rescued and qualified to tell my story.

We don't need a degree to be qualified storytellers in God's eyes; He rewrites our shame stories with His grace-filled stories. Because He rewrites our stories, He qualifies us with the identity we have through His Son. His rewrites eliminate any areas shame wants to use to disqualify us.

AN INVITATION TO REFLECT

- ❖ What does "Qualified" mean to you right now?
- ❖ How is shame keeping you from embracing this idea of being qualified?
- ❖ How can knowing you are qualified reframe shame's grip on your identity?

AN INVITATION TO PRAY

Abba Father, I will give thanks to You for qualifying me. Let me see that purpose in the good works You established for me. May I be courageous to be vulnerable to share my story so that others can see shame has no place at Your table. Amen.

AN INVITATION TO PAUSE

How does understanding this characteristic of your identity in Christ change your place setting at the table?

My Notes

DAY 8

Forgiven

*If we confess our sins,
he is faithful and just to forgive us our sins
and to cleanse us from all unrighteousness.*
1 John 1:9

Sometimes I read a verse and can identify with it immediately, while other times I struggle with it. The same can be said about the identity we have in Christ. *Forgiven* is a name I can sink my teeth into easily. We have been taught since we were small that God forgives us, but sometimes we stumble in forgiving others. I think that in order to understand *forgiven*, we need to look at forgiveness too.

Shame-based identities often cannot see how forgiveness is even possible. I suffered with this thought for a number of years. Having been raped in a church, I struggled with the location of the rape more than the rape itself. When I told my mother, she told me I asked for it, and as a result, her response sealed my shame. I struggled to see how God could love me or forgive me.

Yes, I was an innocent victim when a friend took advantage of me, but my sin came in the choices I made after it happened. Even though I tried to return to God, the rape made me hold faith at a distance, which allowed shame to take ahold of me and keep me from seeing things clearly. I buried the event for years. If I didn't admit it, then it didn't happen, right? It was only years later that I would accept that date rape exists.

Shame asks questions like "How could God forgive me for _____?" "How could God love me when I did _____?" or "How could I forgive them for what they did?" But Scripture answers this in Luke 23:34 (NIV) where Jesus said, "Father, forgive them, for they do not know what they are doing." I cannot say for sure that my rapist did not know what he was doing, but I do know he saw nothing wrong with it. It's possible my mother did not understand the ramifications her words had on me. But I can learn to forgive like Christ when I follow His lead.

As we endeavor to forgive like Christ, it is important to understand we must fully embrace God's forgiveness before we can fully forgive others. Part of that is remembering that God does not forgive like we do and He has the ability to truly leave our offenses in the past (Hebrews 8:12). We are forgiven simply by asking for forgiveness. This confession and, in turn, repentance, allows us to live fully forgiven, which allows us to forgive others.

AN INVITATION TO REFLECT

- ❖ What does being fully forgiven mean to you right now?
- ❖ How is shame keeping you from being fully forgiven?
- ❖ How can accepting forgiveness reframe the identity you have rooted in shame?

AN INVITATION TO PRAY

Abba Father, knowing You forgive me for my sins is humbling. Knowing You can forgive others for the pain they have caused is amazing. Teach me to forgive like Jesus did on the cross even when it feels impossible. Help me to see forgiveness sets me free. Amen.

AN INVITATION TO PAUSE

How does understanding this characteristic of your identity in Christ change your place setting at the table?

My Notes

DAY 9

Loved

*For God so loved the world, that he gave his only Son,
that whoever believes in him should not perish but have eternal life.*
John 3:16

I have struggled most of my life with love. When my father would strike out in anger, I did not have anyone brave enough to stand up for me. The same can be said of my mother who used shame to control me. Words like "You could be so pretty," or "Mind in gear before mouth in motion," caused me to doubt my appearance and my intelligence.

But God's love doesn't shame us. His love is pure and unconditional. It was only my experience that led me to attach conditions to love, especially knowing when I failed to meet those conditions, love was often removed. Whether those who forged this in me were conscious of their role, I don't know, but it shaped how I would see love apart from God. Although showing love can be challenging at times as an adult, a child loves until they are taught differently. A child also craves the security love brings. But adults who have unhealed wounds from their lives cannot always love a child in a healthy way.

When we think of love, it is often as a construct built by the world. We place value on gifts, physical appearances, and wealth. God just loves. It is that simple. He created the earth in all its beauty for us. He provided a variety of things to sustain us—vegetables, fruits, meat, and so on.

"'For my thoughts are not your thoughts, neither are your ways my ways' declares the LORD. 'As the heavens are higher than the earth, so are my ways higher than your ways and my thoughts than your thoughts'" (Isaiah 55:8-9 NIV). We must remember His love is not like our love. While our love is limited, His love is not.

AN INVITATION TO REFLECT

- What does the name "Loved" mean to you right now?
- How is shame keeping you from embracing being loved by God?
- How can knowing you are fully loved reframe your shame identity?

AN INVITATION TO PRAY

Abba Father, I am so thankful that You do not limit Your love for me. Sometimes, Lord, I cannot understand how You can love me, but I thank You for the simplicity of Your love. You truly amaze me. Help me to love others like You love me: unconditionally and without reservation. Amen.

AN INVITATION TO PAUSE

How does understanding this characteristic of your identity in Christ change your place setting at the table?

My Notes

DAY 10

Known

> *For you formed my inward parts;*
> *you knitted me together in my mother's womb. I praise you,*
> *for I am fearfully and wonderfully made.*
> *Wonderful are your works; my soul knows it very well.*
> *My frame was not hidden from you, when I was being made in secret,*
> *intricately woven in the depths of the earth.*
> *Your eyes saw my unformed substance; in your book were written,*
> *every one of them, the days that were formed for me,*
> *when as yet there was none of them.*
> Psalm 139:13–16

Growing up, I was known as Lester's little sister. I relished that identity. I felt like somebody until that identity was no longer valid. When my brother died, I had lived thirty years as his little sister. Before his death, some of his friends took to calling me "sister," a name that made me feel special, loved, and accepted. I had no need for a new identity as long as I was *his* little sister.

Since my life revolved around my family, my worth came from them. Even though I was constantly put down by my mother, I still found myself trying to gain her approval. But when my brother died, my world turned upside down, and I no longer had a place of belonging. His friends stopped calling, and it took me years to discover I had placed my identity in my role within my nuclear family. As those who knew me within that role disappeared one by one, I felt lost and alone.

I needed the identity my family provided because I could not see myself as God did. My parents had friends, whom I adopted as my friends. My brother had friends, whom I claimed as my own. But as each one went to heaven, God unrooted that identity so I could allow Him to work on changing what it meant to be truly known. Little by little, I found myself turning more and more to Him, and I came to accept that He not only knew me, but He also provided for me.

When our identities are placed in the wrong thing, shame wins by distracting us with the wrong kind of identity. Shame-based identities are temporary and unhealthy. But when we have our identities rooted in Christ, then we find security within that role, knowing it will never waver, falter, or change.

AN INVITATION TO REFLECT

❖ What does the thought of being known by God mean to you right now?

❖ How is shame distracting you from embracing being fully known?

❖ How can the name "Known" reframe your shame?

AN INVITATION TO PRAY

Abba Father, living within the truth that You know me and love me anyway makes me feel held by You. You know my heart. You know my pain. You know the desire to be free from the pain of the past. You are El Roi, the God who sees me and, therefore, who *knows* me. Thank you for loving me just as I am. Amen.

AN INVITATION TO PAUSE

How does understanding this characteristic of your identity in Christ change your place setting at the table?

My Notes

DAY 11

Secure

> *I am sure that neither death nor life, nor angels nor rulers,*
> *nor things present nor things to come, nor powers,*
> *nor height nor depth, nor anything else in all creation,*
> *will be able to separate us*
> *from the love of God in Christ Jesus our Lord.*
> Romans 8:38–39

Rejection is a powerful experience and can happen as early as infancy. In my case, premature birth began a cycle of rejection. Born two months before my due date, I stayed in the hospital for another thirty days while my mother went home. Instead of my mother's arms, I was in an incubator, missing out on the bonding that occurs during those first few weeks of life. As a result, my mother often told others I did not want affection as an infant.

Because I was underdeveloped at birth, I also had a heightened awareness of sound and touch. I was born a highly sensitive person with attention deficient disorder, and as such, my whole being could not handle the tightness of a hug. This led to even greater insecurity as I was unable to experience in childhood the very thing that communicates love and protection.

For some of us, finding security in God's love is not an easy journey. Because we feel rejected when we disappoint others, we feel their disappointment in the way they seem to remove their love from us. But God's love is not based on our actions. He already knows we are going to screw up before we even think that thought. Because God's love is not based on anything we can do or not do, it stands up to the shame we carry.

Even when shame says we are unlovable, God rebukes that shame, "Be gone, you are not welcome in my beloved's life." It is that truth that can help us overcome ugly and unkind words from others. And we can fully rest in knowing God's love holds us and brings us securely into His tight embrace.

AN INVITATION TO REFLECT

- ❖ What does the idea of being secure in Christ mean to you right now?
- ❖ How is shame keeping you from knowing the true grace of being secure in Christ?
- ❖ How can the name "Secure" reframe your shame?

AN INVITATION TO PRAY

Abba Father, the way You love me is beyond my understanding. I get so caught up in the *whys* and the *hows* of love that I often limit the love I can receive. Thank You for not setting limits on Your love. Remind me I am securely held by You, my Abba Father. Amen.

AN INVITATION TO PAUSE

How does understanding this characteristic of your identity in Christ change your place setting at the table?

My Notes

DAY 12

Redeemed

*You have taken up my cause, O Lord;
you have redeemed my life.*
Lamentations 3:58

Whenever I hear the word *redeemed*, I cannot help but think of a coupon. In isolation, a coupon is a worthless piece of paper. Its only value comes from the place (or person) who issued it. To be redeemed, the coupon must be presented, and a purchase made. In many respects, we are coupons in God's eyes. The purchase was made by Christ, and we have value because of the price He paid. While His gift is available to everyone, shame often convinces us we hold no value.

When I have felt worthless, it has most often been because I made someone else of more value than myself. I learned from an early age that my opinion was not as important as others'. Part of a dysfunctional family is that there is a center of that family that the other members revolve around. "Keep *that* person happy" is a common motto within a dysfunctional family. My father was my mother's knight, and he defended her no matter how wrong she was. He was powerless to her manipulation (silent treatment, stop eating, stop talking, etc.). As for me, my value came last within our family dynamic, and I had no defender of my own.

We appeared to be the perfect Christian family from the outside looking in. But the truth was, it was this misperception that prevented me from understanding redemption and led me to develop a destructive self-loathing. In that destructive mindset, I became suicidal and followed through with an attempt, and yet, God redeemed my failed attempt into an understanding of suicidal thoughts so that I can help others. I talk openly about my attempts in the hope I can help others see it takes more than a decision in Christ. It takes a relationship with Him in order to restore hope.

Are we redeemed? Yes, by the blood of Christ we are redeemed. But our stories are also redeemed by God for a purpose. We have value because He says we are valuable.

AN INVITATION TO REFLECT

- ❖ What does "Redeemed" mean to you right now?
- ❖ How is shame keeping you from living as one who is redeemed?
- ❖ How can knowing you are redeemed help reframe your shame?

AN INVITATION TO PRAY

Abba Father, thank You for loving me more than I can love myself. I will forever praise Your name because You redeemed me. Show me every day how to embrace being redeemed. Remind me Your thoughts are not my thoughts. Help me see myself as You do. Amen.

AN INVITATION TO PAUSE

How does understanding this characteristic of your identity in Christ change your place setting at the table?

My Notes

DAY 13

Coheir of God

> *The Spirit himself bears witness with our spirit that we are God's children, and if children, then heirs— heirs of God and fellow heirs with Christ, provided we suffer with him in order that we may also be glorified with him.*
> Romans 8:16-17

Inheritance is something you are born into, and in some cases, the value can be substantial. When my parents died, I inherited an abundance of stuff. I barely had time to grieve my mother before my father died weeks later, and all at once, I inherited debt, a gift shop, cars, and their houses. It was as though my whole identity changed in a matter of thirty days. First, in becoming motherless, and then an orphan. While the loss and grief were overwhelming, it struck me that the *stuff* I inherited was like my parents, only temporary.

At the time of my mother's passing, I was singing in a choir and in the process of learning a new song. In the chorus, a line spoke the truth that with God, there are no orphans. The first time we sang its refrain, I crumbled as the meaning struck me while grieving the loss of my mother. She was gone, and I was left without her. But my faith once again told me God was right there. My Abba Father would never leave me or forsake me.

Shame tells us we do not matter, we do not belong, and our value is debatable. But God says we are His children, and our inheritance one day will be the glory of God. All we suffer here will be used to glorify God, and we get to share in that as His heirs. Our inheritance is our place in heaven with our Father. His place is our place, and His glory is our glory—what a wonderful inheritance.

AN INVITATION TO REFLECT

- What does being called "Coheir of God" mean to you right now?
- How is shame keeping you from embracing your role as the coheir of God?
- How can embracing being a coheir of God reframe the identity shame has built in you?

AN INVITATION TO PRAY

Abba Father, Your love amazes me. It is everlasting and more valuable than anything earth could provide. Thank You for providing me with a rich and lasting inheritance. Continue to show me my value to You and my place *with* You. Amen.

AN INVITATION TO PAUSE

How does understanding this characteristic of your identity in Christ change your place setting at the table?

My Notes

DAY 14

Never Alone

*Be sure of this: I am with you always,
even to the end of the age.*
Matthew 28:20 (NLT)

My mother raised me to believe family is the most important thing in this world. A favorite saying of hers was, "After all, when friends leave, all you have left is family." And following her advice, I put family before everything. But in doing so, when they died, they took my identity with them.

One by one my family left me, and yet I never felt alone. This is likely because feeling lonely and feeling alone are two entirely different things. But shame does play one against the other. Shame wants us to feel that no one cares, and more pointedly, that God doesn't care. Shame tells us we are alone and we do not belong anywhere, which can completely isolate us from the truth of who God is.

Scripture teaches us that God is always with us (Immanuel). Instinctually, I knew God was with me from the age of eleven. Yes, I have a story that is darkened with suicide attempts and rape, but my story doesn't stay in that darkness. My story of shame is changed by the light of God, who has not left me because of the choices I have made or were made for me. It is because my story is darkened with those horrible events that I have felt God's presence more during those trials than at other times in my life, and shame has not won.

Our loving Father provides reminders in Scripture of His presence in our lives. "The LORD is close to the brokenhearted and saves those who are crushed in spirit" (Psalm 34:18 NIV). This verse repeats to our souls every time we feel low, "God is right here." God provides Scripture so that we know who He is and how He loves us. God loves us and shows that love by being present in our lives daily, whether in times of feast or famine.

AN INVITATION TO REFLECT

- What does "Never Alone" mean to you right now?
- How is shame keeping you from embracing the thought that you are never alone?
- How can knowing God is ever-present reframe your shame?

AN INVITATION TO PRAY

Abba Father, You are my loving Father. You are always with me, seeing everything, and still loving me through it *all*. What a comfort it is to know I am never truly alone, even if I feel very alone. Thank You for Your constant presence. What an amazing Father You are to me. Amen.

AN INVITATION TO PAUSE

How does understanding this characteristic of your identity in Christ change your place setting at the table?

My Notes

DAY 15

Treasured

You are a people holy to the LORD your God,
and the LORD has chosen you to be a people for his treasured possession,
out of all the peoples who are on the face of the earth.
Deuteronomy 14:2

For someone who struggles with value and worth, seeing myself as being among the most treasured of God has been a challenge. Rejection and shame can leave one feeling devoid of any kind of worth. The preferential treatment of my brother over me was a constant reminder that I was not enough. Add to it a friend group in school including everyone else but me, I saw it as one more place to feel worth-less-than others.

No wonder I could not understand the concept of being treasured or feel it could ever apply to me. My worth was based on others' opinions. Comparison also played a huge part in my shame-based identity. I learned to compare myself to others because others held more value than I did. I placed others and their opinions before me. By doing so, I came to think God did the same thing.

As a result, my thinking about God became flawed. I was restricting Him to the tiny worthless box I'd built for myself. First Samuel 16:7 reveals a truth that counters that restriction: "But the LORD said to Samuel, 'Do not look on his appearance or on the height of his stature, because I have rejected him. For the LORD sees not as man sees: man looks on the outward appearance, but the LORD looks on the heart.'" We often think of God in our own human ways. But God is not restricted to our ways; He sees the past, present, and future all at once. This verse shows us that God is looking at our hearts, and we cannot see what is in the hearts of others.

Shame wants us to only relate to the things that keep us rooted in the pain of the past. It will use comparison and lies to accomplish that goal. There is no place for God in a shame-based identity because we focus instead on the limited view of other people's opinions. My shame companion was faulty because of the importance I put on others' opinions. Someone else had more value than me because they belonged in the ways I deemed important.

Treasured means there is value, a sense of belonging to someone. In this case, we belong to God and He treasures us. It's really that simple. He sees us (El Roi). He knows our stories. And He treasures us all the more.

AN INVITATION TO REFLECT

❖ What does "Treasured" mean to you right now?
❖ How is shame keeping you from embracing the name "Treasured"?
❖ How can knowing you are treasured reframe your shame?

AN INVITATION TO PRAY

Abba Father, the truth that You treasure me is at times hard to accept and understand. In the past I could not think about being treasured. So thank you for helping me to see my value was established by You long before I was even born. Amen.

AN INVITATION TO PAUSE

How does understanding this characteristic of your identity in Christ change your place setting at the table?

My Notes

DAY 16

Adopted

> *All who are led by the Spirit of God are sons of God.*
> *For you did not receive the spirit of slavery to fall back into fear,*
> *but you received the Spirit of adoption as sons,*
> *by whom we cry, "Abba! Father!"*
> Romans 8:14–15

"God gave me the wrong family!" This thought never consciously crossed my mind. But I did find myself drawn to other mothers because of the poor connection I had with mine. And as a result, God gifted me over the years with some godly women who modeled a love I only dreamed of in my childhood.

When we are presented with the name "Adopted," it leaves some of us confused and others overjoyed. *Adopted* can be seen in Scripture when we are referenced as "sons" (see Galatians 4:4–7 and 1 John 3:1). Christ used "brothers and sisters" in Matthew 25:40 (NIV). These few verses show a true sense of family with God as the Father, Christ as our brother. Shame often forces us to believe we have no place, no real family. But God wants us to know He is a loving Father, one who claimed us and adopted us into His fold. No one can take that away. We belong. We have a place.

In Romans, we see the use of "Abba Father," which is a less formal name for God the Father. *Abba* means *Daddy*. The use of Abba shows a more intimate relationship a son would have with his Father. We are called into that more intimate relationship with God because He called us "sons." When we seek a deeper relationship with God, we feel we know Him and He knows us. It is in the "knowing" that we have the desire to be less formal with Him. We give Him the privilege of being called "Abba Father."

Shame wants us to keep to a formal relationship. It says distance is better. It takes trust to obtain a more personal relationship, and shame says don't trust. Trust means vulnerability and the loosening of shame's grip.

AN INVITATION TO REFLECT

❖ What does it mean to you to be called "Adopted"?
❖ How is shame keeping you from embracing the name "Adopted"?
❖ How do you think knowing you're adopted can reframe who you think you are in Christ?

AN INVITATION TO PRAY

Abba Father, You amaze me when I think of all the ways you have shown your love to me. I am adopted by *You* because you knew I needed a Father who loved me without condition. Thank You for the family I have received in being a part of the family of Christ. Amen.

AN INVITATION TO PAUSE

How does understanding this characteristic of your identity in Christ change your place setting at the table?

My Notes

DAY 17

Equipped

*All Scripture is breathed out by God and profitable for teaching,
for reproof, for correction, and for training in righteousness,
that the man of God may be complete, equipped for every good work.*
2 Timothy 3:16–17

I started writing a blog in 2018. Not long after I began, I found myself doubting my abilities. The longer I wrote, the more shame had an ugly hand on me as I battled with my thoughts. *Who wants to read this?* From there, it was a snowball effect that finally ended when I stopped writing. I found myself having moments like Moses, coming up with every excuse I could to keep from doing what God called me to do.

Shame told me I was not qualified or equipped to write a blog, a book, or even a letter. My mother planted seeds of doubt in me at an early age, often calling me stupid. In high school, I wrote until I heard some classmates making fun of me and my writing. Those experiences made it difficult for me to embrace the calling I felt from God. I knew He wanted me to write, but self-doubt was destructive to the creative process.

But as I tried to answer that call, I found myself looking to Scripture more and more as I started writing. I prayed over the words I knew were formulating in my heart. I listened for God's direction (my own direction became preachy). I started writing blogs knowing God instructed every word. He equipped me for every good work (blog). When we rely on God for inspiration and instruction, He equips us beyond our abilities—as Hebrews

13:21 (NLT) says, "May he equip you with all you need for doing his will." Just like Moses, God gives us all gifts so that we can bring Him glory.

AN INVITATION TO REFLECT

- ❖ What does "Equipped" mean to you right now?
- ❖ How is shame keeping you from embracing that He calls us "Equipped"?
- ❖ How can "Equipped" reframe your shame identity?

AN INVITATION TO PRAY

Abba Father, You are the caller of people, the giver of everything we need. I need to trust You more in the calling You have placed on my life. Thank You for equipping me with intention. Use me to show others how You have also equipped them. Amen.

AN INVITATION TO PAUSE

How does understanding this characteristic of your identity in Christ change your place setting at the table?

My Notes

DAY 18

Made Whole

> *May God Himself, the God who makes everything holy and whole, make you holy and whole, put you together—spirit, soul, and body— and keep you fit for the coming of our Master, Jesus Christ."*
> 1 Thessalonians 5:23–24 (MSG)

While shame tells us we are unworthy and broken, God's word says otherwise. Because I believed what shame told me I was, I could not embrace who God says I am, and as a result, I devalued myself for many years. Doing so kept me rooted in those beliefs by showing me all the ways I "was not." I compared myself to others thinking that God also works the same way. I even discredited "good" things because shame made me feel undeserving of anything good.

Part of the healing process from the trauma I carried as a result of the shame inflicted on me during my childhood is seeing myself through different lenses. The shift has been a slow process and has required deep soul work. In one workshop I attended on trauma, a simple phrase changed my perspective: Just as I am.

> *Just as I am*
>   *God loves me.*
> *Just as I am*
>   *I belong.*
> *Just as I am*
>   *I have a purpose.*
> *Just as I am*

I am secure.
Just as I am
I am perfect.
Just as I am
I am invited.
Just as I am
I am special.
Just as I am
I am worthy.
Just as I am
I am enough.
Just as I am
I am deserving.

Shame tells us the opposite of each of these lines. Shame convinces us we are broken and need to be fixed before we can experience one of these "I am" statements. But we can see ourselves as whole, set apart as holy, because God loves us just as we are (nothing more and nothing less).

AN INVITATION TO REFLECT

❖ What does "Made Whole" mean to you right now?
❖ How is shame keeping you from embracing that you are made whole in Christ?
❖ How can embracing God-breathed wholeness reframe your shame?

AN INVITATION TO PRAY

Abba Father, my identity should come from you, but I have looked to others to define me instead. Show me how my true identity and self-worth are only found in You. You gifted me with blessings I see as an identity. You have made me whole; no longer do I need to search for the incomplete part of me. You complete me. You love me, just as I am. Amen.

AN INVITATION TO PAUSE

How does understanding this characteristic of your identity in Christ change your place setting at the table?

My Notes

DAY 19

Strong

*He said to me, "My grace is sufficient for you,
for my power is made perfect in weakness."
Therefore, I will boast all the more gladly about my weakness,
so that Christ's power may rest on me.
That is why, for Christ's sake, I delight in weaknesses, in insults,
in hardships, in persecution, in difficulties.
For when I am weak, then I am strong.*
2 Corinthians 12:9–10 (NIV)

When my parents died so close together, I was left in shock and a state of constant grief. But even in my weakened state of grief, my faith became strong. Paul's writings in 2 Corinthians made sense to me during those days. Whereas before I could not understand, "For when I am weak, then I am strong," that season forced me to turn to God for support, which strengthened my faith. The key was *where* I turned for that support.

When I tried to do it alone, I stayed in a state of weakness. My faith was in me and my abilities instead of God's. But during a time of immense grief, God gifted me with a church community that rallied around and supported me. With four houses and one large business to take care of, I often felt alone and overwhelmed in the task of resolving my parents' estate, and my childhood wounds left me feeling I had no place in this world.

With both parents gone before I could resolve any wounds that they had inflicted, I felt lost. Shame said I needed an apology or an explanation to heal, which kept me rooted in a state of misery. I had so much to grieve that I couldn't grieve and wanted to do nothing but hide, which led to a season of isolation.

"When I am weak, then I am strong" was not yet in my vocabulary, but God provided a way for me to be strong. My church community not only lifted me up; they also held me up. A friend came to my house and made me come to Bible study with her and a group of other ladies, and joining them saved my life. It was also during this time I discovered the gift of writing again. There was no way that I could have gone through the losses I suffered without the community God brought me.

The faithfulness of God is shown best when we feel weak, physically or mentally. During the times we feel weak, He provides ways to strengthen us, and sometimes He does so by using others to pour into our lives. He provides renewed hope to face another day when we do not feel quite ready to do so.

AN INVITATION TO REFLECT

❖ What does "Strong" mean to you right now?
❖ How is shame keeping you from embracing the strength available even in your weakness?
❖ How can the name "Strong" help you reframe your shame?

AN INVITATION TO PRAY

Abba Father, Your faithfulness is revealed to me when I seek You to make me strong, whether in my spiritual health, my mental health, or my physical health. You provide the strengthening power through Your Spirit. Help me to remember I am strong because You make me so. This is just another way You show me how much You love me. Thank You for all the ways you love and strengthen me. Amen.

AN INVITATION TO PAUSE

How does understanding this characteristic of your identity in Christ change your place setting at the table?

My Notes

DAY 20

Holy

As he who called you is holy, you also be holy in all your conduct, since it is written, "You shall be holy, for I am holy."
1 Peter 1:15–16

When I focus on my sins, shame sets in. When shame sets in, then I see myself as anything but holy. I use words that are not of Christ, continuing to berate myself, and then just give up trying, leaving myself to utter, "Why bother?" Sound familiar? Shame loves this mindset. But God says we have been set apart, and because we are *His*, we are holy.

Holy is defined as

1. dedicated to religious use; belonging to or coming from God; consecrated; sacred
2. spiritually perfect or pure; untainted by evil or sin; sinless; saintly
3. regarded with or deserving deep respect, awe, reverence, or adoration

Even though there are a number of definitions for *holy*, not all are accurate. Personally, it has been hard for me to pinpoint a good definition. I seem to miss the mark, but understanding the definition is just part of understanding this identity. We are holy because that is how God sees us when we accept the salvation Jesus offers us through his death on the cross and resurrection three days later. God set us apart from the world (do not be of this world) to do good works for Him. But what does that really mean?

It means He called us, and we are His. He set us apart within the world to be different from the world. This is one of the reasons we have a hard time being called holy. Living in the world, we see as the world does. And yet He set us apart from the world by calling us to be like Him. We are to be His examples, but it is important to remember we won't always get it right. Even when we slip up, we can return to God, forgiven and securely loved.

AN INVITATION TO REFLECT

- ❖ What does "Holy" mean to you right now?
- ❖ How is shame keeping you from embracing the call to be holy?
- ❖ How can being named "Holy" help you reframe your shame?

AN INVITATION TO PRAY

Abba Father, You are holy, and because You have called me so, I am holy as well. Help to transform my view of *holy* to reflect being dedicated to You. And may I be set apart from the world in all that I say and do. Amen.

AN INVITATION TO PAUSE

How does understanding this characteristic of your identity in Christ change your place setting at the table?

My Notes

DAY 21

Citizen of Heaven

*Our citizenship is in heaven,
and from it we await a Savior, the Lord Jesus Christ.*
Philippians 3:20

Our feelings often lead us places we don't expect to go. But knowing we have a place in eternity should run deeper than anything else. It is a place we earned only by accepting the invitation of Christ. No works play a part in our place in heaven. We only have to do one thing: accept.

I have long searched for my place in this world. Changed jobs, changed community groups at church, the list could go on and on. For years, I could not understand why I felt I did not fit in. It was because I had embraced the lie that I did not belong anywhere. The truth is, I never trusted anyone enough to allow myself to truly belong. I found myself questioning the name "Citizen of Heaven," wondering if my citizenship was guaranteed. However, the day I said yes to my Savior is the day my future was secured. Because my future is secured, then I can find rest in the hope that brings.

Two verses bring clarity to the meaning behind this identity. Philippians 3:20 gives us a hope for the future in Christ as our Savior. Ephesians 2:19 furthers that hope in taking away some identities we have and countering them with our place among others: "So then you are no longer strangers and aliens, but you are fellow citizens with the saints and members of the household of God." Both verses provide hope in different ways.

The day you were born you became a citizen of a country. You did nothing but breathe to earn your citizenship. It is the same with being a citizen of heaven. We have already established that shame says we do not belong, we have no place, we do not fit in. This is why Ephesians resonates so strongly when considering this piece of our identity in Christ.

Shame keeps us as strangers and aliens—meaning foreigners, nomads in a sense. We search for a place to belong, but until we lessen shame's grip, we will continue to wander and wonder. We have a place secured by Christ for us, but we must keep our eyes fixed on Him.

AN INVITATION TO REFLECT

- ❖ What does being named a "Citizen of Heaven" mean to you right now?
- ❖ How is shame keeping you from embracing the name "Citizen of Heaven"?
- ❖ How can being called a citizen of heaven reframe your shame?

AN INVITATION TO PRAY

Abba Father, You give me peace of mind that I have citizenship in Your household. It is secure and it is mine, not because of anything I did but everything that Christ did for me. What a blessing to know where I will be when I close my eyes to this world. Amen.

AN INVITATION TO PAUSE

How does understanding this characteristic of your identity in Christ change your place setting at the table?

My Notes

DAY 22

Cared For

"Casting all your anxieties on him, because he cares for you."
1 Peter 5:7

Intense emotional pain was the storm that was brewing in my teenage years. It is also what made me think the world would be better off without me. I just wanted the heartache to stop, the teasing to stop, the ostracizing to stop. I wanted to be different so that I could be something special. Years of hearing how I didn't measure up or what was wrong with me took its toll. I was not emotionally equipped to handle all my story held.

Feeling devalued by others caused me more pain than I could handle. I had no one in my life I could talk to about what was causing the pain. Only God was there, and I talked to Him constantly, but I often failed to find Scriptures that would have made a difference.

As a result, shame led me to believe life was no longer worth living. My loved ones would no longer have to make excuses for me. And so, in my teenage years, I attempted suicide. But in a strange mercy, the towel bar I attempted to use to hang myself broke, hitting me in the head with a force that struck me to my core. My suicide attempt had been thwarted, and God used the very thing I was using to end my life as a wake-up call.

Scripture tells us that storms will come into our life, but we have a God who gave us the ultimate life jacket in His Son because He cares for us. Shame wants us to believe we are unable to handle those storms, but God says we are capable because He is our rock and our firm foundation. He is also the shield protecting us from those storms.

Shame lies to us, whispering words of doubt as to who we are and what we can withstand. But God whispers to us, "I am here, and I will not leave you."

Shame will try to tell us we are alone and no one cares, but the cross shows us just how much He cares.

AN INVITATION TO REFLECT

- ❖ What does "Cared For" mean to you right now?
- ❖ How is shame keeping you from embracing being cared for by Christ?
- ❖ How does knowing you are cared for reframe who you think you are in Christ?

AN INVITATION TO PRAY

Abba Father, You are my shield when I feel weak in the storms. You give me a firm place to stand and a life jacket to carry me to shore. You show me just how much You care for me by protecting me from myself. You showed me how much You care for me by sending Your Son to die for my sins. Thank You for caring for me in all the ways I need. Amen.

AN INVITATION TO PAUSE

How does understanding this characteristic of your identity in Christ change your place setting at the table?

My Notes

DAY 23

Reconciled

*For if while we were enemies we were reconciled to God
by the death of his Son, much more, now that we are reconciled,
shall we be saved by his life.*
Romans 5:10

I was a bookkeeper who drove my boss crazy. When it came to reconciling the accounts, I would chase a penny. The books had to be perfectly reconciled, or I was not satisfied. He would tell me to plug it and move on, but I couldn't do it. As I have explored being reconciled as a God-breathed identity, I always return to that penny and the parable of the lost sheep.

Matthew 18:10–14 tells the story of the lost sheep:

See that you do not despise one of these little ones. For I tell you that in heaven their angels always see the face of my Father who is in heaven. What do you think? If a man has a hundred sheep, and one of them has gone astray, does he not leave the ninety-nine on the mountains and go in search of the one that went astray? And if he finds it, truly, I say to you, he rejoices over it more than over the ninety-nine that never went astray. So it is not the will of my Father who is in heaven that one of these little ones should perish.

My penny is my own version of the lost sheep. I had to reconcile the penny, or I could not sleep. Shame would have sided with my boss—plug it in with the amount I was out and decide it is not worth finding. In every way, shame tells us that *we* are not worth finding. And while the experience may be different, the end result is the same. We are left to feel unworthy.

Yes, we are lost without Christ. But God determines our value the day we are born. If He is the One to determine our value, then why do we allow others to change that value? My friend, allow me to tell you that shame, just like fear, is a liar. God values us and desires us to be reconciled to Him through the blood of Christ. If no one ever told you that you were worthy, allow me to tell you now. You are worth more now than anyone else's "worth-less."

AN INVITATION TO REFLECT

- ❖ What does "Reconciled" mean to you right now?
- ❖ How is shame keeping you from embracing the name "Reconciled"?
- ❖ How can being called "Reconciled" reframe any shame you feel?

AN INVITATION TO PRAY

Abba Father, thank You for each identity we have through Your Son. Help me to see myself in all that means for me. Loosen my hands so that I may release the shame keeping me stuck in a worth-less state. Help me see myself as worthy of You finding me. Amen.

AN INVITATION TO PAUSE

How does understanding this characteristic of your identity in Christ change your place setting at the table?

My Notes

DAY 24

Valuable

Are not two sparrows sold for a penny?
And not one of them will fall to the ground apart from your Father.
But even the hairs of your head are all numbered.
Fear not, therefore: you are of more value than many sparrows.
Matthew 10:29–31

When I was in third grade, my parents received word from the school that I had failed the vision test and needed a follow-up with an optometrist. During the exam, the doctor kept saying how fuzzy the world must look to me. I thought he was a little crazy when he mentioned his daughter being able to see individual leaves on the tree. But when I got my first pair of glasses, I understood and saw exactly what he meant. Before my glasses, the trees were green blobs; then, after my glasses, clear crisp images of individual leaves.

Establishing our worth is difficult because in large part, we are seeing our worth through the eyes of others. Changing that view of ourselves is like changing glasses. We must begin with an examination if we are to ever see the change with our own eyes. The same process can be applied to our identities. As we examine our identities in Christ, we need to filter out the fuzzy parts, the areas not of God.

The filter we use against these impurities is the total understanding of who we are in God's eyes through the identities explored here. Scripture applied to perspective allows us to line up those identities against God's vision of who we are. Once we filter out those impurities (untrue beliefs), then we have a new vision of who we are through the "Christ filter." This is how God sees us. When we root our worth here, we can start to heal our shame-based identity.

AN INVITATION TO REFLECT

- ❖ What does "Valuable" mean to you right now?
- ❖ How is shame keeping you from seeing yourself as valuable?
- ❖ How can knowing you are valuable reframe any future shame?

AN INVITATION TO PRAY

Abba Father, when I see your creation, let me be reminded of how much You value me. Strengthen my vision and open my eyes to who I am in Christ instead of seeing through the lens of past hurts and judgments. You do great things; please do them in me. Amen.

AN INVITATION TO PAUSE

How does understanding this characteristic of your identity in Christ change your place setting at the table?

My Notes

DAY 25
More Than Conquerors

No, in all these things we are more than conquerors through him who loved us.
Romans 8:37

Defeat was a common experience for me growing up. I could not stand up for myself out of fear of the punishment that would befall me if I did. Even the closest mothers and daughters struggle while the younger one is becoming independent. So naturally, my mother and I should have had disagreements. But if I did or said anything that she took offense to, then I had to answer to my father. Defeat grew deeply here.

My father, when protecting my mother, went to extremes. He instilled fear with one glance. This fear prevented me from learning how to defend myself. Years later, I would understand that I had suffered emotional abuse from her and physical abuse from him. But fear of voicing any abuse kept me from seeking help. Their deaths freed me from some of that learned fear. But I still struggled with this identity for years, because how could I be "more than" when my experience whispered I was "less than"?

To be more than conquerors, we must start by identifying what being a conqueror entails. A deep dive into words relating to *conqueror* led me to a favorite song by a favorite artist, "Overcomer" by Mandisa. When we overcome something, we do not need to continue to look back at that which was defeated. I could not identify with this because shame did not allow me to see myself in the light of Christ. He defeated this shame, and consequently, if I abide in Him and He in me, then I can truly begin to see myself as a conqueror.

Fear often keeps us from trying to do battle. Shame keeps us in a fearful place, too afraid to find our voice. But Christ gives us a voice by showing us fear and shame have no place with Him. Scripture replaces the lies that we cannot defeat, telling us both who we are and whose we are. In this, we can stand beside Him who loves us and declare our conquering status.

AN INVITATION TO REFLECT

- ❖ What does being "More Than Conquerors" mean to you right now?
- ❖ How is shame keeping you from seeing yourself as more than a conqueror?
- ❖ How can knowing you are more than a conqueror shift your focus and reframe your shame?

AN INVITATION TO PRAY

Abba Father, what a joy it is to count myself as more than a conqueror. It is an identity that brings to mind an overcoming power and hope. I can overcome the weight I have been carrying in my shame-based identity, for You see me as a warrior, more than a conqueror. And I will praise you. Amen.

AN INVITATION TO PAUSE

How does understanding this characteristic of your identity in Christ change your place setting at the table?

My Notes

DAY 26

Child of God

> *You are no longer foreigners and strangers,*
> *but fellow citizens with God's people*
> *and also members of his household.*
> Ephesians 2:19 (NIV)

I grew up in a Southern Baptist church, which resulted in its own shame wounds. Because I did not fit a certain mold, I felt like an outcast. As I look back on that chapter of my story, I see now the dysfunction in my own family colored how I thought church should be and still shades it today. Every time we went to church, we would magically become the perfect family. But behind that mask of perfection was a different story. It never occurred to me that others wore the same mask.

Dysfunctional is an ironic word when we apply it to God's children. The very definition describes His chosen people in Exodus, who did not operate normally or properly. But that is the beauty of being in God's family. We cannot do life without one another, because together we find strength, even with some growing pains. We also find a way to grow in God's love. For those who find themselves unlovable, it is hard to stay in the community of others. But when we find others like us, there's a connection that expands our sense of family.

We are all looking for that place where we belong. But for those of us with a heavy presence of shame, we doubt every place we look. In the end, we try to create a place of belonging when we marry and start our families. And yet, there still seems to be something missing even here, within our family unit. Our place of belonging comes through the community and family provided by our churches.

The moving parts of God's kingdom are made up of uniquely gifted people, like you and me. And God's kingdom needs us to embrace that invitation instead of isolating ourselves due to uninvited perceptions. When we isolate, we actively remove our part in the community of believers. Will the church survive without us? Yes. But it is not what God intended.

AN INVITATION TO REFLECT

- ❖ What does being a child of God mean to you right now?
- ❖ How is shame keeping you from embracing the name "Child of God"?
- ❖ How can being a child of God help reframe your shame?

AN INVITATION TO PRAY

Abba Father, thank You for giving me a chance to be connected with other children of Yours. Help me to stay connected to others so that I can experience Your love. Please remind me of the fullness that this name will bring in the fellowship of the uniquely different children You have claimed. Amen.

AN INVITATION TO PAUSE

How does understanding this characteristic of your identity in Christ change your place setting at the table?

My Notes

DAY 27

Ambassador

*We are ambassadors for Christ, God making his appeal through us.
We implore you on behalf of Christ, be reconciled to God.*
2 Corinthians 5:20

When I was in college, I went on summer missions. I was thrilled to go, and the experience was a mixture of wonderful and not-so-great. I was assigned to a church in St. Louis, and I had a partner from another state. But I had not lived a clean college life before going to St. Louis.

After I returned home, I was determined to live a life worthy of being a missionary, only to fail miserably. My mother, being my mother, said words that I had already wrestled with, but hearing them from someone else just sealed my shame: "Some missionary you are." Those four words made me hesitate to tell anyone that I went on any kind of mission trip. In time, my language looked more like a sailor than a child of God.

When we look at our lives through the lens of shame, the identity of *ambassador* may cause us to shake our heads. Shame looks only at what feeds it, and those parts can make us feel less than others and balk at the identity. Shame asks the question, *Why would God consider me to be His ambassador?*

But God sees us through the lens of Christ, made clean and holy by His blood. It does not excuse our sin, but it does cover that sin in its cleansing power and allows us to see ourselves as ambassadors. God uses us and every ugly bump *we* see to bring others back to Him. We are the carriers of His words to others to help them see their way back to Him, and in doing so, we are ambassadors of reconciliation.

AN INVITATION TO REFLECT

- ❖ What does the name "Ambassador" mean to you right now?
- ❖ How is shame keeping you from embracing who you are meant to be as an ambassador of Christ?
- ❖ How do you think your role as an ambassador will help reframe shame you feel in the future?

AN INVITATION TO PRAY

Abba Father, thank You for seeing me differently than I see myself. It amazes me, thrills me, and excites me to become more. Take all my life "bumps" and use them for *Your* glory. Show me how I can be the ambassador you need in me. Amen.

AN INVITATION TO PAUSE

How does understanding this characteristic of your identity in Christ change your place setting at the table?

My Notes

DAY 28

Gifted

*As each has received a gift, use it to serve one another,
as good stewards of God's varied grace; whoever speaks,
as one who speaks oracles of God;
whoever serves, as one who serves by the strength that God supplies—
in order that in everything God may be glorified through Jesus Christ.
To him belong glory and dominion forever and ever. Amen.*
1 Peter 4:10–11

Regardless of what we were made to believe about ourselves, God has given us a variety of gifts, both spiritual gifts and natural talents. While you may have doubts about your gift because of the negative things said, your gift will remain yours whether you share it or not. I started writing a little poetry in high school, along with a few short stories. I submitted a piece for a competition, but instead of receiving accolades, I found myself the butt of a joke by my peers judging the submissions. So I laid my pen down and only told stories in my head where no one else could touch them.

Then, as an adult, I wrote something for a friend, who said I had a gift. It was the first time I had ever heard those words from anyone. I was encouraged to share my writing with others and received the same encouragement. It was then I felt God's call on me to write.

Even though shame wants us to ignore our calling, sharing our talents loosens shame's grip. Friends have a way of letting us know what we are good at, our natural God-given gifts. So if you are struggling to find that gift, ask a close friend for their input. Scripture is the road map to help us discover our spiritual gifts, and the encouragement of godly friends can help point the way to our God-given talents.

Spiritual gifts are those found in Scripture (mercy, administration, etc.; see Romans 12:6–8) and are designed to build the kingdom. Our natural gifts and talents can be used along with our spiritual gifts to build the kingdom too. I write and share my writing to point others to the hope we have in Christ. I also love to cook, and I share that gift with friends who need cheering up. I have a friend who is gifted with the voice of an angel, and she uses her gift to lead worship. This is a good place to journal answers to the questions "What areas am I gifted in?" and "How can I use this gift to bless others?"

AN INVITATION TO REFLECT

- ❖ What does the name "Gifted" mean to you right now?
- ❖ How is shame keeping you from embracing the call to use those gifts?
- ❖ How do you think embracing the name "Gifted" can reframe your shame?

AN INVITATION TO PRAY

Abba Father, I stand in the glory of the universe You created, humbled at the magnitude of it. Its colors leave me awestruck. I see Your creativity and am blown away by it. So help me to see the ways You gifted me and how I can use those gifts for You. Amen.

AN INVITATION TO PAUSE

How does understanding this characteristic of your identity in Christ change your place setting at the table?

My Notes

DAY 29

Free

> *And because you are sons, God has sent the Spirit of his Son into our hearts, crying, "Abba! Father!" So you are no longer a slave, but a son, and if a son, then an heir through God.*
> Galatians 4:6–7

My father had an explosive temper. He could backhand me so fast I barely had time to think to move, let alone actually move. The pain of the blow caused tears to start, which brought out more of his temper. He would eventually yell, "Stop crying or I'm going to give you something to cry about!"

This event shows the devaluation I suffered, both emotionally and mentally. Because emotions made my father uncomfortable, he wounded others in his discomfort. Shame was already present in my life, so because I had no one to comfort me (countering the devaluing effect), shame led me to believe I could not trust an otherwise appropriate emotional response.

Shame tells us over time that any abuse we suffer is not as detrimental as we believe. It says we deserve the abuse. But Scripture reminds us we are no longer slaves to that shame. It may have helped shape the story, but Christ's actions changed the story. By conquering the grave, defeating the shame of the cross, and receiving the glory He deserved, he offered us freedom. We are no longer slaves to shame. By acknowledging the trauma we go through, we give ourselves permission to feel and accept we are no longer slaves:

To shame …

To silence ...

To suppressed feelings ...

Instead, we are free to heal.

AN INVITATION TO REFLECT

- ❖ What does being free mean to you right now?
- ❖ How is shame keeping you from embracing the freedom you have in Christ?
- ❖ How does being named "Free" reframe your shame identity?

AN INVITATION TO PRAY

Abba Father, I want to praise You for the grace of freedom and the hope found there. May I fully embrace the freedom I have from the shame I have long felt. Thank You for loving me so much that You gave me a way to trade the identity of slave for freedom. Amen.

AN INVITATION TO PAUSE

How does understanding this characteristic of your identity in Christ change your place setting at the table?

My Notes

DAY 30

Victorious

*Everyone born of God overcomes the world.
And this is the victory that has overcome the world—our faith.*
1 John 5:4

It's time to set the table. When we began, there were three places at a large table, one for Christ, one for you, and one for your shame. Shame's place setting overwhelmed the other two when we began our journey together. But now that we have re-rooted our identity over the last twenty-nine days, we should have only two places at a much smaller table. The table Christ sets for you is an intimate one that is designed for fellowship.

Shame keeps us from fellowship with others and with Christ. But now we can see ourselves in a new way so that intimacy becomes greater as our shame becomes smaller. As you move forward in your healing journey, I want to encourage you to work through the days again and journal as you go. The first time we read about the names we can claim in the identity of Christ, we may not have grasped how our shame had blinded us to who we are and whose we are.

Journaling through any devotional again is valuable because we often see or feel something new each time, which helps bring about change. Understanding who we are in Christ and how every name God bestows on us can change who we thought we were is pivotal. Remember, shame wants us rooted in the past along with those hurtful moments that may have defined our thinking about ourselves. By the time I studied who I am in

Christ, I only saw how a handful of names made a difference in my life where shame was concerned. However, now that I have studied each one, I see the value in each of them. Journaling about the memories also helped me see any false narratives that I had developed over the years. The beauty of God's Word is that we can revisit the same Scripture and gain new knowledge about God and about our identity in Him.

Victorious means we have overcome, prevailed in a battle and won. Our shame has told us what losers we are, but Christ says we are winners through Him. When we stay in our shame, we stay in a worldview that is tainted. But when we embrace our Christ-given identity, we move into a victorious life colored by love and forgiveness.

AN INVITATION TO REFLECT

- ❖ How have the last thirty days shown you where shame has kept you from being victorious in Christ?
- ❖ How have you overcome shame in the last thirty days and been victorious?
- ❖ Which of the names God bestows upon you has meant the most to you in this journey? Why?

AN INVITATION TO PRAY

Abba Father, we have overcome so much over the last month. This was not easy work, but we prevailed. We have now seen who You say we are through Your Son. Help us to continue to embrace the truth of who we really are. Thank You for each of the identities we have in Christ; without them we would be stuck in a world of shame. Amen.

AN INVITATION TO PAUSE

How does understanding this characteristic of your identity in Christ change your place setting at the table?

My Notes

Conclusion

REFRAME YOUR SHAME

Reframe Your Shame

Congratulations on committing to thirty days of studying your identity in Christ. If you are ready to dig even deeper, take time to review the devotions and explore your own relationship with shame.

When we think of shame, we tend to have an automatic response to it. To reframe it is to intentionally change how we think about and respond to shame and to replace negative self-talk with more positive messages. This is why God led me to write this devotional. I needed to replace the negative self-talk that had shaped my identity with a more positive God-given mindset. The following steps should help you process your shame and reframe it.

As you read the devotions again, journal the following:

❖ What is my negative self-talk?

❖ What memories surround my self-talk?

❖ What if I were to share this with someone else? (Shame wants you to think you cannot share your story because empathy and vulnerability counteract its power.)

❖ What could I say to my younger self whenever this self-talk started that would change it? (e.g., My self-talk is "I'm stupid." I would say, "You are not stupid, but the frustration of someone else is coming out in a statement of negativity.")

- What are your triggers? Are they related to fear? (e.g., I struggle with the fear of abandonment and rejection, and shame kicks in when my fear is activated.)

- How can I replace the self-talk I hear with a more loving self-talk guided by my identity in Christ?

Shame needs secrecy, silence, and judgment to grow. Judgment doesn't always come from others. Self-compassion goes a long way when dealing with shame. Sometimes we need to be a compassionate, empathic friend to ourselves. Consider how you would change your words when speaking to a child. My friend, you are that *child*, and you deserve the same gentleness and grace found in the identity *you* have in Christ!

Grace means that all of your mistakes
now serve a purpose instead of serving shame.
—Brené Brown

My Notes

Questions for Digging Deeper

INTRODUCTION
1. How does it make you feel knowing *we* were on *Jesus's* mind in the hardest moment of His earthly life?
2. How does this change how you see yourself?

DAY 1: NEW CREATION
1. What is keeping you from accepting your *new* identity in Christ?
2. How can you change that binding belief which is keeping you from accepting who you are in Christ?

DAY 2: ACCEPTED
1. How has the world made you feel unaccepted?
2. How does it feel to know that God accepted you before you were born?

DAY 3: ENOUGH
1. How would you define the word *enough*?
2. How does God's grace shift your understanding of the word?

DAY 4: HEARD
1. How does it make you feel when you know your voice is being heard?
2. If you could say anything and know that God hears and understands, what would you say and why?

DAY 5: CHOSEN

They will make war on the Lamb, and the Lamb will conquer them, for he is Lord of lords and King of kings, and those with him are called and chosen and faithful. Revelation 17:14

1. Reading the Scripture above, how do you feel about being chosen?
2. Understanding how shame works, does being called *chosen* challenge you, or are you ready to embrace this identity? Why?

DAY 6: MASTERPIECE

1. Do you see yourself as God's masterpiece? Why or why not?
2. How has shame colored your self-image differently than the one God has for you?

DAY 7: QUALIFIED

1. How has shame convinced you that you are not qualified?
2. How do you now see yourself as qualified?

DAY 8: FORGIVEN

1. How does it feel to know you are forgiven?
2. How has shame kept you from fully accepting God's forgiveness?

DAY 9: LOVED

1. In your life, how do you see God's love?
2. Do you currently feel treasured, secure, and firmly loved? Why or why not?

DAY 10: KNOWN
1. How are you known, especially in the names others call you or by profession?
2. What are some things that keep you rooted in past identities God is trying to uproot with these identities in Christ?

DAY 11: SECURE
1. What makes you feel the most secure in life?
2. How does it make you feel knowing we cannot disappoint God?
3. How does it feel to know that *nothing* can take God's love from us?

DAY 12: REDEEMED
1. How does it feel to be God's favorite coupon, redeemed by the precious blood of His Son?
2. What are the areas in your life where you feel unredeemable? How does knowing who you are in Christ change that for you?

DAY 13: COHEIR OF GOD
1. What holds value to you? What is your inheritance?
2. How does being a coheir with Christ change how you see yourself?

DAY 14: NEVER ALONE
1. Can you think of a time you felt God was not there? What feelings surface when thinking about this time?
2. How has God shown you that you are never really alone?

DAY 15: TREASURED
1. What is your greatest treasure? Why is it of value to you?
2. How do you see yourself as treasured by God?

DAY 16: ADOPTED
1. How has your family shaped your view of what it means to be a family?
2. How does seeing God as a Father change that viewpoint?

DAY 17: EQUIPPED
1. How have you been equipped for what God has called you to do?
2. How has shame played a role in diminishing that calling?

DAY 18: MADE WHOLE
The feeling that we need to be more than or less than is common in a shame-based identity. It is a feeling of incompletion, which leads us to search for the other half or the parts we feel are missing. Think about the ways you have searched for meaning.

1. Have those ways made you feel complete? Are you still searching?
2. How does this identity change how you view the ways you listed?

DAY 19: STRONG
1. Thinking of a difficult time in your life, how was your faith strengthened?
2. How can you use that knowledge to face the difficulties you have today?

DAY 20: HOLY
1. What comes to mind when you hear the word *holy*?
2. How does understanding the true meaning of *holy* change how you see your identity in Christ?

DAY 21: CITIZEN OF HEAVEN
1. How does this name bring you a sense of belonging?
2. How can it change your view of where you fit in?

DAY 22: CARED FOR
1. What does "Cared For" mean to you?
2. How has shame kept you from seeing just how deeply God cares for you?

DAY 23: RECONCILED
1. How has shame kept you from being reconciled with God?
2. How does it feel to know that God Himself determined your value long before you were created?

DAY 24: VALUABLE
1. In what areas do you find value in your life?
2. In what areas do you need help finding your value?

DAY 25: MORE THAN CONQUERORS
1. How would you define the word *conqueror*?
2. In what areas do you need to see yourself as *more than*?

DAY 26: CHILD OF GOD
1. Have you ever thought about the connection you offer others?
2. How does that change your view of yourself?

DAY 27: AMBASSADOR
1. How does being an ambassador of God change the person you see in the mirror's reflection?
2. What are some "bumps" you see that may need some adjustment to see yourself as an ambassador?

DAY 28: GIFTED
Examine your life for a minute, thinking of some of the natural abilities God gave you. These could be writing, drawing, singing, caring for children or the elderly, cooking, playing a sport, or even working at a certain profession.

1. How could you use that gift to glorify God?
2. How does knowing your spiritual gifts change your perception of self?

DAY 29: FREE
1. How has shame kept you in bondage?
2. What are some areas where you can see shame's grip on your identity? What would freedom look like to you in these areas?

DAY 30: VICTORIOUS
1. What memories have surfaced in the last thirty days that connect to the shame you currently carry? How has this journey helped you process that shame?
2. What name that you own as a part of your identity in Christ has meant the most to you and why?

Endnotes

Day 18: Made Whole

In the ESV translation of 1 Thessalonians 5:23, "completely" is used—not partially but completely. I chose The Message translation because it oversimplifies Paul's writing without changing the meaning. The key in these verses is God and His power at work to make us sanctified (set apart as holy).

Day 20: Holy

Collins Dictionary, "holy," accessed February 5, 2025, https://www.collinsdictionary.com/dictionary/english/holy.

Day 28: Gifted

If you are curious about different spiritual gifts and what they mean, download the "Description of Spiritual Gifts" from College Church at https://college-church.org/impact/serve/. For a free evaluation of your spiritual gifts, see https://redletterchallenge.com/discover-your-spiritual-gifts.

ORDER INFORMATION

To order individual copies go to
redemption-press.com/bookstore

For discounts on bulk orders
send an email to
bookorders@redemption-press.com.
subject: bulk orders

www.ingramcontent.com/pod-product-compliance
Lightning Source LLC
LaVergne TN
LVHW011802240725
816720LV00004B/18